EMMANUEL JOSEPH

The Third Pillar, How Social Science Informs Political and Business Strategy

Copyright © 2025 by Emmanuel Joseph

All rights reserved. No part of this publication may be reproduced, stored or transmitted in any form or by any means, electronic, mechanical, photocopying, recording, scanning, or otherwise without written permission from the publisher. It is illegal to copy this book, post it to a website, or distribute it by any other means without permission.

First edition

This book was professionally typeset on Reedsy.
Find out more at reedsy.com

Contents

1 Chapter 1   1

1

Chapter 1

Chapter 1: The Interconnection of Society, Politics, and Business The triad of society, politics, and business forms the foundation upon which the modern world is built. These three pillars are deeply intertwined, each one influencing and being influenced by the others. Social science serves as a lens through which we can understand these interconnections and navigate the complexities of our world. By examining societal trends, cultural norms, and human behavior, social science provides valuable insights that can inform political strategies and business decisions. It helps us to see beyond the immediate and obvious, revealing the underlying patterns and dynamics that shape our societies.

Social science teaches us that politics and business are not isolated entities but are embedded within the social fabric. Political decisions impact business environments, just as business practices can influence political landscapes. For example, a government's regulatory policies can create a favorable or challenging environment for businesses, while corporate lobbying and campaign contributions can shape political agendas and outcomes. Social science helps us to understand these interactions and to anticipate the potential consequences of political and business strategies.

Furthermore, social science emphasizes the importance of considering the human element in political and business strategies. It reminds us that policies and business decisions ultimately affect people's lives and well-being.

By incorporating insights from social science, policymakers and business leaders can develop strategies that are not only effective but also socially responsible and ethical. This approach can lead to more sustainable and equitable outcomes, benefiting both society and the economy.

In conclusion, the interconnection of society, politics, and business is a fundamental aspect of our world. Social science provides the tools and perspectives needed to understand these interconnections and to navigate the complexities they present. By incorporating social science insights into political and business strategies, we can create more informed, effective, and responsible approaches to the challenges and opportunities we face.

Chapter 2: The Role of Culture in Shaping Political and Business Strategies Culture plays a crucial role in shaping political and business strategies. It encompasses the shared values, beliefs, norms, and practices that define a society and influence the behavior of its members. Understanding the cultural context is essential for developing strategies that are relevant and effective in a given environment. Social science provides the framework for analyzing and interpreting cultural dynamics, helping us to understand how culture influences political and business decisions.

In the political realm, culture shapes the preferences and behaviors of voters, politicians, and policymakers. It influences the issues that are prioritized, the policies that are proposed, and the ways in which political campaigns are conducted. For example, in societies where individualism is highly valued, political strategies may emphasize personal freedom and individual rights. In contrast, in collectivist cultures, strategies may focus on community well-being and social harmony. Social science helps us to identify these cultural patterns and to develop strategies that resonate with the values and beliefs of the target audience.

Similarly, in the business world, culture affects consumer preferences, employee behavior, and organizational practices. Companies that understand the cultural context in which they operate can develop products, services, and marketing strategies that align with the values and expectations of their customers. For instance, a business operating in a culture that values sustainability and environmental responsibility may adopt eco-friendly practices and promote their green credentials. Social science provides the tools for analyzing cultural trends and for developing business strategies that are culturally informed and relevant.

Moreover, culture influences the ways in which political and business actors interact with each other. It shapes the norms and expectations for negotiation, collaboration, and conflict resolution. By understanding the cultural context, political and business leaders can navigate these interactions more effectively and build stronger relationships with their counterparts. Social science offers insights into the cultural dimensions of these interactions and helps leaders to develop culturally sensitive and effective strategies.

In summary, culture is a critical factor in shaping political and business strategies. Social science provides the framework for understanding cultural dynamics and for developing strategies that are culturally informed and relevant. By incorporating cultural insights into their strategies, political and business leaders can enhance their effectiveness and achieve better outcomes.

Chapter 3: The Impact of Social Networks on Political and Business Strategies Social networks play a significant role in shaping political and business strategies. These networks encompass the relationships and connections between individuals, groups, and organizations. They serve as channels for the flow of information, resources, and influence, and they can have a profound impact on political and business outcomes. Social science provides the tools for analyzing social networks and for understanding their dynamics and effects.

In the political realm, social networks can influence voter behavior, political mobilization, and policy outcomes. For example, political campaigns often rely on social networks to spread their messages and to mobilize supporters. Grassroots movements leverage social networks to build momentum and to advocate for change. Policymakers use their networks to gather information, to build coalitions, and to negotiate agreements. Social science helps us to map and analyze these networks, revealing the key actors, relationships, and pathways of influence.

In the business world, social networks can affect a wide range of activities, from marketing and sales to innovation and collaboration. Businesses use social networks to reach potential customers, to gather market intelligence, and to build brand loyalty. They also rely on networks to collaborate with partners, to access new technologies, and to drive innovation. Social science provides the tools for understanding the structure and dynamics of these networks, helping businesses to leverage their connections for strategic advantage.

Moreover, social networks can shape the interactions between political and business actors. For instance, lobbying efforts often rely on networks of relationships to gain access to policymakers and to advocate for specific policies. Similarly, public-private partnerships depend on the networks between government agencies and businesses to coordinate their efforts and to achieve their objectives. Social science helps us to understand these interactions and to develop strategies for navigating and leveraging social networks.

In conclusion, social networks are a powerful force in shaping political and business strategies. Social science provides the tools for analyzing these networks and for understanding their dynamics and effects. By incorporating insights from social network analysis, political and business leaders can develop more effective and informed strategies, leveraging their connections to achieve their goals.

Chapter 4: The Role of Identity and Group Dynamics in Political and Business Strategies Identity and group dynamics are critical factors in shaping political and business strategies. Identity encompasses the various attributes, beliefs, and affiliations that define individuals and groups, while group dynamics refer to the interactions and relationships within and between groups. Social science provides the framework for understanding these concepts and for analyzing their impact on political and business behavior.

In the political realm, identity plays a key role in shaping voter preferences, political mobilization, and policy outcomes. For example, political parties often appeal to specific identity groups, such as ethnic, religious, or socioeconomic groups, to build their support base. Social movements leverage identity to mobilize individuals around a common cause or goal.

Policymakers consider the identity of their constituents when developing policies and proposals. Social science helps us to understand the role of identity in politics and to develop strategies that resonate with the values and beliefs of different identity groups.

Group dynamics also play a significant role in political behavior. For instance, the interactions and relationships within political parties, coalitions, and interest groups can influence decision-making processes and policy outcomes. The dynamics of group polarization and groupthink can affect the behavior and decisions of political actors. Social science provides the tools for analyzing group dynamics and for developing strategies that navigate and leverage these dynamics effectively.

In the business world, identity and group dynamics influence consumer behavior, employee interactions, and organizational practices. Companies that understand the identities of their customers can develop products, services, and marketing strategies that align with their values and preferences. Similarly, understanding the group dynamics within an organization can help managers to build effective teams, to foster collaboration, and to drive innovation. Social science provides the tools for analyzing identity and group dynamics and for developing business strategies that are informed by these insights.

Moreover, identity and group dynamics can shape the interactions between political and business actors. For example, corporate social responsibility (CSR) initiatives often consider the identity of stakeholders and aim to build positive relationships with different identity groups. Public-private partnerships may navigate group dynamics to achieve their objectives. Social science helps us to understand these interactions and to develop strategies that are informed by identity and group dynamics.

In summary, identity and group dynamics are critical factors in shaping political and business strategies. Social science provides the framework for understanding these concepts and for analyzing their impact on political and business behavior. By incorporating insights from social science, political and business leaders can develop more effective and informed strategies that resonate with the identities and dynamics of their target audiences.

Chapter 5: The Influence of Social Norms and Values on Political and Business Strategies

Social norms and values play a pivotal role in shaping political and business strategies. Social norms are the unwritten rules and expectations that guide behavior within a society, while values are the deeply held beliefs that underpin these norms. Understanding these cultural elements is essential for developing strategies that are both effective and socially responsible. Social science provides the tools for analyzing social norms and values and for understanding their impact on political and business behavior.

In the political realm, social norms and values influence voter behavior, policy preferences, and political discourse. For example, social norms regarding gender roles and equality can shape the priorities and platforms of political parties and candidates. Values such as justice, freedom, and solidarity can influence public opinion and policy outcomes. Social science helps us to identify and analyze these norms and values, providing insights into the cultural context in which political strategies are developed and implemented.

Similarly, in the business world, social norms and values affect consumer preferences, organizational practices, and corporate reputation. Companies that align their strategies with the prevailing norms and values of their target markets can build stronger relationships with their customers and enhance their brand loyalty. For instance, businesses operating in cultures that value sustainability and environmental responsibility may adopt green practices and promote their commitment to these values. Social science provides the tools for understanding these cultural elements and for developing business strategies that resonate with the values and expectations of consumers.

Moreover, social norms and values shape the interactions between political and business actors. For example, corporate lobbying efforts may be influenced by norms regarding transparency and social responsibility. Public-private partnerships may be shaped by values such as trust, cooperation, and mutual benefit. Social science helps us to understand these interactions and to develop strategies that are aligned with the prevailing norms and values.

In summary, social norms and values are critical factors in shaping political and business strategies. Social science provides the tools for analyzing these cultural elements and for understanding their impact on behavior. By incorporating insights from social science, political and business leaders can develop strategies that are culturally informed, socially responsible, and effective.

Chapter 6: The Role of Communication and Media in Political and Business Strategies Communication and media play a vital role in shaping political and business strategies. They serve as the primary channels for conveying information, shaping public opinion, and influencing behavior. Social science provides the framework for analyzing communication processes and media dynamics, helping us to understand their impact on political and business outcomes.

In the political realm, communication and media are essential tools for engaging with voters, shaping policy debates, and building political support. Political campaigns use various communication strategies to convey their messages, mobilize supporters, and persuade undecided voters. Media outlets, including traditional media and social media platforms, play a crucial role in shaping public opinion and framing political issues. Social science helps us to analyze these communication processes and to develop strategies that are effective in reaching and engaging the target audience.

Similarly, in the business world, communication and media are critical for marketing, branding, and customer engagement. Businesses use communication strategies to promote their products and services, build brand loyalty, and manage their reputation. Media channels, including advertising, public relations, and social media, are used to reach potential customers and to influence their purchasing decisions. Social science provides the tools for analyzing communication and media dynamics, helping businesses to develop strategies that are effective and impactful.

Moreover, communication and media shape the interactions between political and business actors. For example, corporate lobbying efforts often involve strategic communication campaigns to influence public opinion and to advocate for specific policies. Public-private partnerships may use media channels to promote their initiatives and to build support among stakeholders. Social science helps us to understand these interactions and to develop communication strategies that are aligned with the objectives of both political and business actors.

In conclusion, communication and media are critical elements in shaping political and business strategies. Social science provides the framework for analyzing these processes and for understanding their impact on behavior. By incorporating insights from social science, political and business leaders can develop communication strategies that are effective, impactful, and aligned with their goals.

Chapter 7: The Influence of Social Change and Innovation on Political and Business Strategies Social change and innovation are powerful forces that shape political and business strategies. Social change refers to the transformations in societal norms, values, and behaviors over time, while innovation encompasses the development and implementation of new ideas, products, and processes. Social science provides the tools for analyzing these dynamics and for understanding their impact on political and business behavior.

In the political realm, social change can lead to shifts in public opinion, policy priorities, and political alignments. For example, changes in societal attitudes toward issues such as gender equality, environmental sustainability, and social justice can influence the platforms and policies of political parties and candidates. Social movements advocating for change can mobilize public support and drive policy reforms. Social science helps us to understand these dynamics and to develop strategies that are responsive to social change.

Innovation also plays a significant role in shaping political strategies. Technological advancements, for example, can transform the ways in which political campaigns are conducted, enabling new forms of voter engagement and mobilization. Policy innovation can lead to the development of new solutions to societal challenges, enhancing the effectiveness and efficiency of government programs. Social science provides the tools for analyzing innovation processes and for developing strategies that leverage new ideas and technologies.

In the business world, social change and innovation drive market trends, consumer preferences, and competitive dynamics. Companies that are attuned to social change can develop products and services that meet the evolving needs and expectations of their customers. Innovation can lead to the creation of new business models, the development of cutting-edge technologies, and the disruption of established industries. Social science helps us to understand these dynamics and to develop business strategies that are responsive to change and that leverage innovation.

Moreover, social change and innovation shape the interactions between political and business actors. For example, regulatory changes in response to social movements can create new opportunities and challenges for businesses. Public-private partnerships can drive innovation by combining the resources and expertise of government agencies and businesses. Social science provides the tools for analyzing these interactions and for developing strategies that are responsive to social change and that leverage innovation.

In summary, social change and innovation are powerful forces that shape political and business strategies. Social science provides the framework for understanding these dynamics and for developing strategies that are responsive to change and that leverage new ideas and technologies. By incorporating insights from social science, political and business leaders can develop strategies that are adaptive, innovative, and effective.

Chapter 8: The Role of Social Equity and Justice in Political and Business Strategies Social equity and justice are fundamental principles that shape political and business strategies. Social equity refers to the fair distribution of resources, opportunities, and outcomes within a society, while justice encompasses the principles of fairness, equality, and accountability. Social science provides the tools for analyzing these concepts and for understanding their impact on political and business behavior.

In the political realm, social equity and justice are key considerations in the development of policies and programs. Governments have a responsibility to ensure that their policies promote fairness and address social inequalities. For example, policies aimed at reducing poverty, improving access to education and healthcare, and protecting the rights of marginalized groups are informed by principles of social equity and justice. Social science helps us to understand the root causes of social inequalities and to develop policies that promote fairness and justice.

Similarly, in the business world, social equity and justice are important considerations in corporate strategies and practices. Companies have a responsibility to ensure that their operations are fair and inclusive, and that they contribute to the well-being of their employees, customers, and communities. For example, businesses may implement diversity and inclusion programs, adopt fair labor practices, and engage in corporate social responsibility (CSR) initiatives that promote social equity and justice. Social science provides the tools for analyzing these issues and for developing business strategies that are socially responsible and equitable.

Moreover, social equity and justice shape the interactions between political and business actors. For example, public-private partnerships may focus on addressing social inequalities and promoting justice through collaborative initiatives. Corporate lobbying efforts may advocate for policies that promote social equity and justice. Social science helps us to understand these interactions and to develop strategies that are aligned with principles of fairness and accountability.

In conclusion, social equity and justice are fundamental principles that shape political and business strategies. Social science provides the framework for analyzing these concepts and for understanding their impact on behavior. By incorporating insights from social science, political and business leaders can develop strategies that are socially responsible, equitable, and effective.

Chapter 9: The Impact of Globalization on Political and Business Strategies Globalization is a powerful force that shapes political and business strategies. It refers to the increasing interconnectedness and interdependence of the world's economies, societies, and cultures. Social science provides the tools for analyzing the dynamics of globalization and for understanding its impact on political and business behavior.

In the political realm, globalization has led to the emergence of new challenges and opportunities. For example, the increased movement of people, goods, and ideas across borders has created new policy issues related to immigration, trade, and international cooperation. Globalization has also led to the rise of transnational organizations and networks that influence

CHAPTER 1

political decisions and outcomes. Social science helps us to understand these dynamics and to develop strategies that navigate the complexities of the global political landscape.

In the business world, globalization has transformed the ways in which companies operate and compete. Businesses now have access to global markets, supply chains, and talent pools, enabling them to expand their operations and to reach new customers. However, globalization also brings new challenges, such as increased competition, regulatory complexities, and cultural differences. Social science provides the tools for analyzing these dynamics and for developing business strategies that are responsive to the opportunities and challenges of globalization.

Moreover, globalization shapes the interactions between political and business actors. For example, multinational corporations often engage with governments and international organizations to navigate the regulatory environment and to advocate for policies that support their global operations. Public-private partnerships may focus on addressing global issues, such as climate change, poverty, and public health. Social science helps us to understand these interactions and to develop strategies that are effective in the global context.

In summary, globalization is a powerful force that shapes political and business strategies. Social science provides the framework for understanding the dynamics of globalization and for developing strategies that are responsive to its opportunities and challenges. By incorporating insights from social science, political and business leaders can develop strategies that are adaptive, innovative, and effective in the global landscape.

Chapter 10: The Role of Ethics in Political and Business Strategies
Ethics is a critical consideration in shaping political and business strategies. It encompasses the principles of right and wrong that guide behavior and decision-making. Social science provides the tools for analyzing ethical issues and for understanding their impact on political and business behavior.

In the political realm, ethics is essential for ensuring the integrity and accountability of government officials and institutions. Ethical considerations shape the development of policies and programs, as well as the conduct of political campaigns and public administration. For example, ethical principles such as transparency, fairness, and accountability are crucial for maintaining public trust and confidence in government. Social science helps us to understand the ethical dimensions of political behavior and to develop strategies that uphold these principles.

Similarly, in the business world, ethics is important for ensuring the integrity and responsibility of corporate practices. Companies have a responsibility to conduct their operations in a manner that is fair, transparent, and respectful of the rights and well-being of their stakeholders. For example, ethical considerations may guide decisions related to labor practices, environmental sustainability, and corporate governance. Social science provides the tools for analyzing these issues and for developing business strategies that are ethical and responsible.

Moreover, ethics shape the interactions between political and business actors. For example, corporate lobbying efforts may be guided by ethical principles to ensure that they are conducted in a transparent and accountable manner. Public-private partnerships may prioritize ethical considerations to promote the public good and to build trust among stakeholders. Social science helps us to understand these interactions and to develop strategies that uphold ethical principles.

In conclusion, ethics is a critical consideration in shaping political and business strategies. Social science provides the framework for analyzing ethical issues and for understanding their impact on behavior. By incorporating insights from social science, political and business leaders can develop strategies that are ethical, responsible, and effective.

Chapter 11: The Role of Power and Influence in Political and Business Strategies Power and influence are fundamental concepts in shaping political and business strategies. Power refers to the ability to affect the behavior of others and to shape outcomes, while influence involves the ways in which power is exercised and leveraged. Social science provides the tools for analyzing power dynamics and for understanding their impact on political and business behavior.

In the political realm, power and influence shape the decision-making processes and policy outcomes. For example, political leaders and institutions wield power through their authority and resources, while interest groups and lobbyists use influence to advocate for specific policies and to shape public opinion. Social movements and grassroots organizations leverage their collective power to drive social and political change. Social science helps us to understand these dynamics and to develop strategies that navigate and leverage power and influence effectively.

Similarly, in the business world, power and influence shape organizational behavior and market dynamics. For example, corporate leaders and managers wield power through their positions and decision-making authority, while stakeholders such as shareholders, employees, and customers use their influence to shape corporate practices and policies. Competitive dynamics in the marketplace are also influenced by the power and strategies of different businesses. Social science provides the tools for analyzing these dynamics and for developing business strategies that navigate and leverage power and influence.

Moreover, power and influence shape the interactions between political and business actors. For example, corporate lobbying efforts often involve the use of power and influence to advocate for specific policies and to shape regulatory environments. Public-private partnerships leverage the combined power and resources of government agencies and businesses to achieve their objectives. Social science helps us to understand these interactions and to develop strategies that are effective in navigating power dynamics.

In summary, power and influence are fundamental concepts in shaping political and business strategies. Social science provides the framework for analyzing these dynamics and for understanding their impact on behavior. By incorporating insights from social science, political and business leaders can develop strategies that navigate and leverage power and influence effectively.

Chapter 12: The Future of Political and Business Strategies: Integrating Social Science Insights The future of political and business strategies will increasingly depend on the integration of social science insights. As our world becomes more complex and interconnected, the ability to understand and navigate social dynamics will be essential for achieving success. Social science provides the tools and perspectives needed to develop informed, effective, and responsible strategies that address the challenges and opportunities of the future.

In the political realm, the integration of social science insights can enhance the development of policies and programs that are responsive to the needs and aspirations of diverse populations. For example, social science research on issues such as inequality, climate change, and migration can inform the design of policies that promote social equity, environmental sustainability, and human well-being. Social science can also help political leaders to understand and address the root causes of social and political conflicts, fostering more effective and sustainable solutions.

In the business world, the integration of social science insights can drive innovation, competitiveness, and social responsibility. For example, social science research on consumer behavior, organizational culture, and market trends can inform the development of products and services that meet the evolving needs and preferences of customers. Social science can also help businesses to navigate the complexities of global markets, to foster inclusive and diverse workplaces, and to contribute to the well-being of their communities.

Moreover, the integration of social science insights can enhance the collaboration between political and business actors. Public-private partnerships can leverage social science research to address complex social challenges and to promote the public good. Corporate social responsibility initiatives can draw on social science insights to develop strategies that are socially responsible and impactful. Social science can also help to foster trust and cooperation between political and business leaders, enhancing their ability to work together effectively.

In conclusion, the future of political and business strategies will increasingly depend on the integration of social science insights. Social science provides the tools and perspectives needed to understand and navigate the complexities of our world, to develop informed and effective strategies, and to promote social equity, environmental sustainability, and human well-being. By incorporating social science insights, political and business leaders can enhance their ability to address the challenges and opportunities of the future and to create a better world for all.

Chapter 13: The Role of Social Capital in Political and Business Strategies Social capital refers to the networks, relationships, and trust that exist within a society, and it plays a crucial role in shaping political and business strategies. Social science provides the tools for analyzing social capital and for understanding its impact on political and business behavior.

In the political realm, social capital influences voter behavior, political engagement, and policy outcomes. For example, communities with high levels of social capital may experience higher voter turnout, greater civic participation, and more effective governance. Social movements and advocacy groups often rely on social capital to mobilize supporters and to build coalitions. Social science helps us to understand these dynamics and to develop strategies that leverage social capital for political success.

In the business world, social capital affects organizational performance, employee engagement, and customer loyalty. Companies with strong social capital can foster a positive organizational culture, enhance collaboration and innovation, and build trust with customers and partners. For example, businesses that invest in building relationships with their stakeholders can create a loyal customer base and a motivated workforce. Social science provides the tools for analyzing social capital and for developing business strategies that leverage these relationships.

Moreover, social capital shapes the interactions between political and business actors. For example, public-private partnerships often rely on social capital to build trust and to facilitate cooperation between government agencies and businesses. Corporate social responsibility initiatives may focus on building social capital within communities to enhance their impact. Social science helps us to understand these interactions and to develop strategies that leverage social capital for mutual benefit.

In summary, social capital is a critical factor in shaping political and business strategies. Social science provides the tools for analyzing social capital and for understanding its impact on behavior. By incorporating insights from social science, political and business leaders can develop strategies that leverage social capital for success.

Chapter 14: The Impact of Demographics on Political and Business Strategies Demographics refer to the statistical characteristics of populations, such as age, gender, ethnicity, and socioeconomic status. These characteristics play a significant role in shaping political and business strategies. Social science provides the tools for analyzing demographic trends and for understanding their impact on political and business behavior.

In the political realm, demographics influence voter behavior, political preferences, and policy priorities. For example, younger and older voters may have different policy preferences and voting patterns. Demographic changes, such as population aging or increasing diversity, can also impact political dynamics and electoral outcomes. Social science helps us to understand these trends and to develop strategies that are responsive to the needs and preferences of different demographic groups.

In the business world, demographics affect market trends, consumer behavior, and organizational practices. Companies that understand demographic trends can develop products and services that meet the needs of their target markets. For example, businesses may tailor their marketing strategies to appeal to specific age groups, genders, or ethnicities. Demographic changes can also create new opportunities and challenges for businesses, such as the growing demand for healthcare services due to population aging. Social science provides the tools for analyzing demographic trends and for developing business strategies that are responsive to these changes.

Moreover, demographics shape the interactions between political and business actors. For example, public policies that address demographic challenges, such as workforce diversity or population aging, can impact business environments and create new opportunities for collaboration. Corporate social responsibility initiatives may focus on addressing the needs of specific demographic groups to enhance their social impact. Social science helps us to understand these interactions and to develop strategies that are responsive to demographic trends.

In summary, demographics are a critical factor in shaping political and business strategies. Social science provides the tools for analyzing demographic trends and for understanding their impact on behavior. By incorporating insights from social science, political and business leaders can develop strategies that are responsive to demographic changes and that leverage these trends for success.

Chapter 15: The Role of Education and Human Capital in Political and Business Strategies Education and human capital are essential factors in shaping political and business strategies. Human capital refers to the skills, knowledge, and capabilities of individuals, which are developed through education and training. Social science provides the tools for analyzing the impact of education and human capital on political and business behavior.

In the political realm, education influences voter behavior, political engagement, and policy outcomes. For example, higher levels of education are associated with greater political awareness, civic participation, and support for democratic values. Education also plays a critical role in shaping policy priorities, such as investments in education and workforce development. Social science helps us to understand the impact of education on political behavior and to develop strategies that promote educational attainment and human capital development.

In the business world, human capital is a key driver of organizational performance, innovation, and competitiveness. Companies that invest in the education and training of their employees can enhance their productivity, creativity, and adaptability. For example, businesses may implement workforce development programs, offer tuition assistance, and provide opportunities for professional growth. Social science provides the tools for analyzing the impact of human capital on business outcomes and for developing strategies that leverage education and training for success.

Moreover, education and human capital shape the interactions between political and business actors. For example, public policies that promote education and workforce development can create a skilled labor force that benefits businesses and the economy. Public-private partnerships may focus on addressing skills gaps and promoting lifelong learning. Social science helps us to understand these interactions and to develop strategies that leverage education and human capital for mutual benefit.

In conclusion, education and human capital are essential factors in shaping political and business strategies. Social science provides the tools for analyzing the impact of education and human capital on behavior. By incorporating insights from social science, political and business leaders can develop strategies that promote educational attainment, human capital development, and organizational success.

Chapter 16: The Influence of Technology and Digital Transformation on Political and Business Strategies Technology and digital transformation are powerful forces that shape political and business strategies. Digital transformation refers to the integration of digital technologies into all aspects of society and the economy. Social science provides the tools for analyzing the impact of technology and digital transformation on political and business behavior.

In the political realm, technology influences voter behavior, political engagement, and policy outcomes. For example, digital platforms and social media have transformed the ways in which political campaigns are conducted, enabling new forms of voter engagement and mobilization. Technology also plays a critical role in shaping policy priorities, such as investments in digital infrastructure and cybersecurity. Social science helps us to understand the impact of technology on political behavior and to develop strategies that leverage digital transformation for political success.

In the business world, technology and digital transformation drive innovation, competitiveness, and organizational performance. Companies that embrace digital technologies can enhance their productivity, efficiency, and customer engagement. For example, businesses may adopt e-commerce platforms, implement digital marketing strategies, and leverage data analytics for decision-making. Social science provides the tools for analyzing the impact of technology on business outcomes and for developing strategies that leverage digital transformation for success.

Moreover, technology and digital transformation shape the interactions between political and business actors. For example, public policies that promote digital innovation and infrastructure development can create new opportunities for businesses and the economy. Public-private partnerships may focus on addressing digital divides and promoting digital literacy. Social science helps us to understand these interactions and to develop strategies that leverage technology and digital transformation for mutual benefit.

In summary, technology and digital transformation are powerful forces that shape political and business strategies. Social science provides the tools for analyzing the impact of technology on behavior. By incorporating insights from social science, political and business leaders can develop strategies that leverage digital transformation for success.

Chapter 17: The Role of Public Opinion and Perception in Political and Business Strategies Public opinion and perception play a critical role in shaping political and business strategies. Public opinion refers to the collective attitudes and beliefs of a population, while perception involves the ways in which individuals interpret and understand information. Social science provides the tools for analyzing public opinion and perception and for understanding their impact on political and business behavior.

In the political realm, public opinion influences voter behavior, policy priorities, and electoral outcomes. For example, political leaders and parties often rely on public opinion polls to gauge the preferences and concerns of their constituents and to develop campaign strategies. Public perception of political issues and candidates can shape the outcomes of elections and policy debates. Social science helps us to understand the dynamics of public opinion and perception and to develop strategies that are responsive to the views and preferences of the public.

In the business world, public opinion and perception affect consumer behavior, brand reputation, and market dynamics. Companies that understand public opinion can develop products, services, and marketing strategies that resonate with their target audience. Public perception of a company's brand, values, and practices can influence customer loyalty and purchasing decisions. Social science provides the tools for analyzing public opinion and perception and for developing business strategies that are responsive to these dynamics.

Moreover, public opinion and perception shape the interactions between political and business actors. For example, corporate lobbying efforts may be influenced by public opinion on regulatory issues, while public-private partnerships may seek to address public concerns and build trust among stakeholders. Social science helps us to understand these interactions and to develop strategies that are aligned with public opinion and perception.

In conclusion, public opinion and perception are critical factors in shaping political and business strategies. Social science provides the tools for analyzing these dynamics and for understanding their impact on behavior. By incorporating insights from social science, political and business leaders can develop strategies that are responsive to public opinion and perception and that enhance their effectiveness and impact.

Book Description: The Third Pillar: How Social Science Informs Political and Business Strategy

In "The Third Pillar: How Social Science Informs Political and Business Strategy," we explore the profound and intricate relationships between society, politics, and business. This enlightening book uncovers the essential role of social science in understanding and navigating these interconnected realms, offering valuable insights for developing informed, effective, and responsible strategies.

Key Topics Covered:

- **The Interconnection of Society, Politics, and Business:** An exploration of how these three pillars influence and shape each other.
- **The Role of Culture:** Understanding how cultural norms and values impact political strategies and business decisions.
- **Social Networks:** Analyzing the power of relationships and connections in influencing political and business outcomes.
- **Identity and Group Dynamics:** Examining how identity and group interactions shape behavior and strategies in politics and business.
- **Social Norms and Values:** Investigating the impact of unwritten rules and deeply held beliefs on political and business practices.

Additional chapters delve into the importance of social capital, demographic trends, education, technology, and public opinion, highlighting how these factors influence political and business strategies. The book also addresses ethical considerations, globalization, social change, and innovation, providing a comprehensive understanding of the forces shaping our world.

By integrating insights from social science, "The Third Pillar" offers a roadmap for political and business leaders to develop strategies that are culturally informed, socially responsible, and effective. This book is an indispensable resource for anyone seeking to navigate the complexities of our modern world and create strategies that promote social equity, environmental sustainability, and human well-being.

Through a blend of academic rigor and practical applications, "The Third Pillar" bridges the gap between theory and practice, offering readers a deeper appreciation of the vital role that social science plays in shaping our political and business landscapes. Whether you are a policymaker, business leader, academic, or simply curious about the world, this book provides the tools and perspectives needed to make informed and impactful decisions.

www.ingramcontent.com/pod-product-compliance
Lightning Source LLC
LaVergne TN
LVHW020509080526
838202LV00057B/6254